How to Conquer Chronic Fatigue Syndrome

How to Conquer Chronic Fatigue Syndrome

(includes extreme states)

Marin Paun

To order additional copies of this book, contact:
Xlibris
1-800-455-039
www.Xlibris.com.au
Orders@Xlibris.com.au
803678

CONTENTS

1.0 Chronic Fatigue Syndrome or (CFS)

CFS is the hardest condition dealt to the human race. Only cancer in the last 2 weeks is harder. It affects between 200 000 and 250 000 in Australia, yet it is not known or even accepted by numerous doctors, especially those with a small practice. Hopefully with this book and others they will change their minds. It affects people of all ages and sex. It also affects children just born. In Hawthorn Victoria, Australia has one center for chronic fatigue for children. There is no centre for adults because it is not recognized. How is it diagnosed? CFS is a complicated disorder characterised by extreme fatigue that cannot be explained by any other underlying medical condition. The fatigue does not improve with rest and may worsen with physical and mental activities.

Chronic fatigue has been known as myalgic encephalomyelitis (ME) and more recently as, systematic exertion intolerance disease (SEID). Personally I would call it chronic fatigue condition because it is a condition of the system. Any way whatever you call it, it is still the same condition. The cause of chronic fatigue seems to be unknown. Theories start with viral infections to psychological stress. In fact there is none of that, and people who know do not tell, or they seem to be small among the doctoral fraternity. In the best case they do not worry.

So, what causes chronic fatigue? Is it viral infections? Some people develop CFS after viral infections. So maybe some viruses might trigger the disorder. There is physical chronic fatigue, where the absence of some chemical in the body does not create the flow of energy through the system. E.g.: estrogen low in the body following a pregnancy. This is from a friend of mine, who has gone through this situation and spent years with CFS living without energy. She was discovered by accident and cured. The chronic fatigue discussed here is system chronic fatigue, not the chemical which we leave to the doctors to find out what chemical is missing. Another factor which is believed to influence the formation of chronic fatigue is Immune System Problems. People who have chronic fatigue have a weakened or impaired immune system. Is this enough to cause the disorder? The immune system requires a level of energy to function.

Other factors which are thought to have an influence are: hormonal imbalances. Hormones produced in the pituitary gland, adrenal glands and hypothalamus are influential. The level of hormones which are high is believed to have an influence on CFS. Is it possible that when low in energy the hormones are at a different level? The weaker immune system is the result of chronic fatigue, the energy to function is not there, not the other way around. CFS is spread across the society. It is believed that people in their 40's and 50's have it more, but it is an inaccurate result of a survey. Women have more CFS but they expressed it better than males, if you want to make a comparison and not be sexist.

The tragedy is that little children get it and it is hard to improve on their condition. I am also a bit ignorant when it comes to CFS in children. It must be very hard to get them well if they are not adults. It is also believed that stress might trigger CFS, but you get stressed when you have little energy and the condition worsens if you need to do an insurmountable amount of things.

Despite all this evidence that CFS exists, there are people who dispute the facts. It exists and it is very important to cure CFS, to cure the chronic fatigue sufferer. It is cold to stay and watch how somebody can suffer so much. As previously mentioned it is the hardest disease for the human race. On the pole of development, you are low if you disbelieve people who are sick. There is so much evidence yet so much disapproval. There are people who were locked up for being sick. They could not function, they could not defend, especially when without energy. The belief was that it was all in your head. With this condition, I was attacked on the street, in the shops, at the chemist, literally everywhere. The government wants to further develop a system in society, where all sick people are cured amongst society and family. Society does not care and family does not know how deal with health problems. If you go through depression and do not learn how to cure it, when the depression reoccurs next time you will not be able to cure it and you will be overwhelmed. This is why you have it, you must know how to deal with it. Having CFS, there are lots of lessons to be learned, one lesson is to manage your energies. Sleeping, doing good jobs, knowing nice friends and to sleep. To do good jobs to have the nice friends, is just an example. I am excluding extreme cases where energy is very low, and you cannot sleep well, for example whenever you are on 3-4 hours of energy a day and the suicide rate is 99%. In Australia there is believed to be between 2000 and 2500 extreme cases of CFS.

So far, we have covered biological cases, where there is a substance in the body missing which does not allow the energies to flow. Also, we have covered 'the system' case, where there seems to be no reason for the condition. What would you say if we all have a battery in the subconscious mind and is, in this case, very low in energy and causes CFS?! Your daily routine would depend on that, meeting people, socialising, going to work etc. This energy in the battery also acts as protection also known as 'Aura'. Thus, because the of the protection properties I will call it 'shield'.

The battery is hard to recharge, and easily loses energy. I lost my energies working in a call center position from where I did not get anything. I lost energy because of the ego nature of the job, my ego was small. It took me a long time to understand the nature of the CFS, where energies were lost and gained and where you can get a relapse. You need to understand the process of gaining and loosing energies. From 6 hours of energy I went to 10 hours and from that I went back to 3 hours and that is an extreme case of CFS. Another definition of CFS from the system point of view is that the battery loses energy and needs to be replenished. There are cases where energy are at 10 hours a day that are not in danger of going to 3 hours, and there are cases of 3 hours which are extreme cases of CFS. In all cases the battery is involved, and needs to be replenished even if it is at ten hours. So, the definition cover all cases, minimum and extreme. All the biological effects, the immune system, blood sample, the condition of the body, are explained by having lower energy in the battery, lower than normal where you run out of energy in a small amount of time.

The above dictates you how you spend your day. What to do when you have energy and what to do when you do not have energy? The answer is that you will stay in bed when you do not have energy and do activities which produce energy and lose energy .e.g.: listen to music, playing an instrument, watching a movie, doing meditation and so on when you do have energy. The condition is difficult to manage because there is no cure and you need to watch your energies each day to have a new amount of energy. This is rebuilding your battery. This will take years and is not an easy exercise. You need to watch your energy and not to go over your limit, If you go over your limit you will lose energy and not gain energy. This will make it harder for you to recover. Actually, it is a very hard exercise, as you could not handle your energy when you were healthy, and you need to manage it at 3 hours. A lot of people spend years with chronic fatigue, and this why it is hard to manage your energies.

In order to see how much energy you have in terms of hours, when you wake up start doing things until you get heavy legs or arms. This is when your energy stops and you have to spend rest of the time in bed. It can be anything from 3 hours to 14 hours.

I have been in this CFC game for 13 years, and that is a long time. The main reason was that I could not find a place with privacy. It is hard to find an affordable home. Let alone a private place. I manage my energies OK, even if my mind is broken into pieces. I have been like that for seven years now. The process of gaining energy is a slow process, it probably takes 4 years under normal conditions to recover fully. Because I am developed it should be 2 or 3 years under normal conditions. If you change through psychology you should gain energy faster. It is very important to cure CFS/ME. First, we are human beings and do not allow someone to lose his or her life. This is the 21st Century and we do not accept that CFS does not exist. CFS exists and recognizing it and not throwing it in the basket of impossible, is important. We know it exists and we need to help and influence the current diagnostic procedure. I might repeat myself but there is more than one way to diagnose chronic fatigue. One way that is most used is the process of elimination, you eliminate a lot of conditions until you remain with chronic fatigue. E.g.: brain damage. People on alcohol get brain damage so if it is not from alcoholism it is from other conditions. I drink only occasionally, I am a social drinker. The trouble with these diagnostic method is that they take long time. It takes 1 ½ years. to diagnose CFS. This is very hard for a person with CFC, 1 and ½ years with CFS without knowing you have it, is a hard and a long time. In this time, you could recover and suffer less pain. In my case I did not know I had chronic fatigue syndrome until the end of 2007. I suffered for 4 years later, then initial contact. If I had been diagnosed quicker maybe I would have recovered quicker, there is also the dimension of pain, 4 more years of pain that should not have been. If you have extreme chronic fatigue the only thing you are asked to do is lift 2 kg of shopping. There is extreme CFS/ME. Extreme CFS is the hardest of CFS. But the diagnosis is quickly done, in comparison with 'standard CFS'. Outside the hours of operations, when you should be in bed, you can ask the patient if he can lift the shopping, and the answer is no. Much quicker than 1 and ½ years. During this period of time you could be well or along your way to recovering. It took me four years to diagnose because I thought I was crazy believing I could cure most of the conditions known to humans. Obviously, that was not the case and I need help from some responsible health professionals.

I should be cautious if I try a small firm of doctors where you get a patient with chronic fatigue every 2 years. There might be a chance that they do not believe in chronic fatigue syndrome They do not know what to do with it. They need to be taught about it. They need to be made aware of the condition of CFC.

Currently in Melbourne Australia there are no CFS clinics, but only one center for children. It started to be recognized but there are no clinics, there should be one clinic for extreme cases and one for 'standard cases'. The lifestyle around chronic fatigue should be taught. The day is smaller, as mentioned and you spend a lot of time in bed. A lot of empowering events will take place, so you can grow e.g.: depression, anxiety, general, social, performance and so on. Acquiring self-esteem will be also be important. This is a long process but is very rewarding. You will be able to make decisions about your life. You will be self-reliant and a responsible member of society. You will even teach people around yourself good things. You will become a positive person in society.

There should be a clinic for extreme chronic fatigue. It is different from a standard one because you will need to master psychology and also, you will need to go through the process of death. Only 10% of the population has been through the process of death. It is sad losing a life and you live your life differently losing the life. You are actually liberated, you live your life differently. You are not scared of losing own your life anymore. I am not going to explain the process of death in details, I leave it up to you.

To go through the process of death you need self-esteem. Self-esteem takes 3 to 4 years to develop, as you can see it is a lengthy task. It is enough time to build self-esteem.

So, the clinic for CFS/ME is a bit more complicated when it comes to deal with the extreme condition. You will need to go through the process of death because there will be situations where your life is under threat. You are also required to become a psychologist for yourself because the interventions in the CFS require urgency that you do not have. You do not have time to go to the psychiatrist and tell him that you are suicidal and would like to commit suicide. You need to move from that state to the state of functioning.

As you can see there is a difference between the 'standard' chronic fatigue and the 'extreme' CFS in terms of clinics and in terms of approaching the condition. The 'standard' CFS is not as bad as the extreme but they are both hard. You are asked to manage your energies when you could not do it while on a full day of energy.

In the 'extreme' case you will need to develop yourself in six months when you would normally do that in 7 years. That is big ask, but it is not impossible. There are people who have been through extreme chronic fatigue, so it is possible. It is a pity they did not build a clinic, so the incoming sick people would not have had to have suffered so much.

There are many books written on the physical manifestation of CFS, so I am not going to get into the physical aspects of CFS. What I want to say is that most of the findings with regards to the physical manifestation were done when people would had been in bed with a low level of energy. Most of the findings occur when people are out of energy and there is no flow through your body. In the period you are active, the first 3 to 4 hours seem to be a normal situation.

How to Cure Chronic Fatigue

The best way to deal with CFS is to tell you what I do every day. You need to have a structure in your daily activities. Everything needs to be been done at the same time. CFS/ME can reoccur It can reoccur because we do not follow the energy level in ourselves. We say it is cured, so now I can do anything. No, it is not cured. It is a duty in our life to watch the energy levels, it is the most important factor in your life to watch the energies levels. Enjoy the 'boring' sleep, do good jobs where you do not lose energies, they are challenging, they pay well and you get your social skills. Surround yourself with nice people from whom you gain energies. If you live with passion, make it balanced, not the same thing. In this way Chronic Fatigue will not reoccur.

Extreme Chronic Fatigue

Extreme cases CFS/ME are known as the worst condition in human beings. If you fall in the category of 3 to 4 hours of energy you are believed to be an extreme chronic fatigue sufferer. You find out when your legs and arms become logs and you cannot move. You can also be on 5 to 7 hours of energy and in danger of becoming extreme by not focusing on energies.

The most important factor in chronic fatigue is loss of sleep, no matter how tired you are you cannot sleep. Sleeping pills are subscribed, but doctors do not want to prescribe them because of addiction properties and also tolerance. Any addiction should be free so you can control it, not the other way around, addiction controls you. This is something which has not entered society and the medical fraternity, we need to learn not to make such a big deal because they are addictive. Not all sleeping pills are addictive. Valium, Temazepan, Mogadon are addictive. Restavit even if it is not a sleeping pill has values for sleep, it is not addictive. I personally think if you enjoy the medicine there is a good chance that you will become addicted. Even with cognitive thinking 'wow this is so good' we must remember it is just a sleeping pill and that does not mean it is good.

I am currently on Valium 5 per day, Seroquel 700 of which 100 are not slow release and 5 melatonin which send me to sleep around the afternoon. The Valium is addictive but I do not believe it affected me so far and the rest are not addictive. As you know every drug has side effects. So, the sooner you get well, the better from the medicinal point of view. If by any chance become addicted you will be able to deal with that.

You should have a room which is dark for sleep. The air should be fresh. The doona has to be exact for the kind of weather outside. If it is too thick then you will perspire and you will not sleep. Try to be calm for one hour before your sleep. Do not listen too hard to rock or uplifting music. You will be too high and not able to sleep (also some energy when required will be good for sleep because the lack of energy will impede on your sleeping). Have loose clothes on you so you are not bothered by them. Very important PRIVACY. You do not want to be disturbed during the night. Have something to eat before you go to sleep, a sandwich, a small snack, because you will be disturbed by being hungry. Go to the toilet before sleep, so you will not be disturbed and break the sleeping cycle.

Sleeping 10 hours and breaking your cycle, is not better than 7 ½ hours without disturbance. Another thing which makes you sleep is walking. Walk 15 minutes per day to get tired and to build your endorphins. It will help you with anxiety as well as with your heart beat. You get 'sleeping pills' and you will be able to go to bed at the same time. There is no biological clock, it moves forward and you eventually you sleep during the day.

Most of your energy you have is from sleep after you found out how much energy you have, do half an hour less of your activities, so you can increase your energies. Do not do more than the limit. You will catch up on energies by trying to get back to your limit. Slowly and slowly your energies will increase every three months. Some people will increase their energy faster, some slower depending on the individual. You will be faster if you have acquired skills in psychology. You will also be supervised by a professional who has knowledge in CFS and can do things straight away. There will be a lot of activities and tasks to be done in addition to psychology. I mentioned a few and you might be able to think of some. We will use music for therapy. Uplifting music recorded from the radio using a digital recorder and then downloaded to a computer to be used for next day is good therapy. Usually music is recorded late at night and then download next morning. I personally use the old fashioned cassette recorder that I have been using for 10 years. I buy cassette recorders and cd players with a radio and with that I can record from. There is a problem when the radios will become digital, so you will need a digital radio with cassette and I do not think this is possible. So, the digital recorder is probably better and I will try to use one myself.

You will record also classic music 60 bits Bach, Strauss, Debussy, Mozart and any music which relaxes. You will also relax when you study or read books. You learn faster and in a balanced way in terms of the brain parts. Instrument playing is also good to express yourself. Any instrument, even if you have not started yet is good. You can start at any age. You can only play to a limit, due to energy constrains, after that you will lose energy and you will not benefit. In the same category comes painting. You can start at any age. Remember it is never too late to do anything. Writing books is also good but you need to have to say something to society. Poetry is also used by some people. Personally, I use guitar and books. Everyone has his own pleasures.

Also, I suggest psychiatry visits because you will need medication for mental condition which will appear. That makes the psychiatrist important. Something which is valid for 'extreme' causes of CFS is that they live in our internal world a lot of the time. This is not the same for 'standard'. We all live in both external and internal worlds but in CFS you spend a few hours of energy in the external world, and the rest in the internal world. The internal world is the psychological world separated from the external world by a wall of energy. If you go outside the hours of energy you will acquire a wall of external world which will be hard to get rid of. This is valid for 'extreme' CFS and not for 'standard one'. You will need to lift the mind using music and uplifting material. I acquired this wall of energy a long time ago and I am still not be able to get rid it. I have also acquired a broken mind which can be put together only by an intense feeling. This intense filling will push one fragment high, so the mind will become one.

One event which belongs to extreme chronic fatigue is the starting of the system. The mind, the brain, your spirit, your body should work together in a rhythm called conditioning. We are going to do that by pushing the body to release energy and endorphins to believe that the system has started. For example with a little bit of energy, like walking one or two minutes more every week and every time you change the rhythm. This will bring the whole system back and you will be able to get your sleep and the biological clock. The above does not apply to 'standard' chronic fatigue.

Diet is very important and applies to the two basic CFS conditions. You need to fill up your fridge every two weeks and to get multivitamins regularly. There is a lot of pain with CFS/Me and food becomes very important in the maintaining energies throughout the body. Because there is Coffee in your system some of the substances might disappear from you. For muscle problems use magnesium, there are 5 types of magnesium, it is good if you use all of them. The pains in your muscles seem to diminish. If there is something missing that will show in your body. It is also good to have a regular check-up for sugar and other problems, once a year. You will have side effects from medicines, like being fat, overweight, too much sugar in your blood etc.

Fitness is another point to take into consideration. I recommend walking every day for 15 minutes or longer if it is possible. It is not possible with 'extreme CFS' if you are thinking about your joints. With krill oil or curcumin, you should be able to alleviate the problem. It is very handy to do, you only open the door. It will balance your hormones, will help you sleep, and control your blood/heart pressure. When you sleep you need to be exhausted, otherwise it is harder to sleep. Find out how much walking you can you do. If you do too much you will use energy, if you do not do it properly will not have the desired effects. Some people use Yoga or Swimming. Try what is best for you. Yoga is good for balance. In CFS you can lose your balance. Swimming does not damage the joints, so there is no problem with the joints.

Now that I am on medication I am able to stay in the queue at the supermarkets, exercise 15 minutes a day, and stay in the queue at the doctors. If, you cannot do any exercise do not do it at all. It is possible that in your current situation you cannot do any. You may need some medication for anxiety, depending on where you are for the moment.

As previously mentioned you will become a master of the internal world, a psychologist, you have no choice, it is mandatory. We are going to use the power of positive thinking, used by a lot of people in 'cognitive therapy' and we will call it self-help. One powerful method of changing your inner rules is to use affirmations. They are present tense, personal and positive sentences. You will also emotionalise them and do them louder in front of the mirror for faster effects. Subconscious minds accept present tense statements, to be happy and have more energy. I say these just before I go to bed:

4X I am happy
4X I feel happy
4X I feel happiness
4X I feel good
4 X I really feel good
4 X I feel great
4 X I feel terrific
4 X I wake up tomorrow and I feel good.
4 X I wake up tomorrow and I feel happy,
4 X I wake up tomorrow and I feel great
4 X I wake up tomorrow and I feel terrific.
4 X I feel wonderful
4 X I believe something wonderful will happen to me tomorrow
4 X I believe something wonderful will happen to me today

The effects of these affirmations or cognitive thoughts because they are mixed, imply they will make you happy, energised and feel good. If you do want to do them and they are too many, just do some. This is an example on how to use good affirmations to programme your subconscious mind. The above affirmations are done just before you go to bed and exactly when you wake up, because the subconscious mind is open to suggestions. I use music between affirmations so I can stay positive and not have my mind run in various places. I use music recorded during the night between 10 pm and 12 am. I have more choice in music at that time than during the day. Music is very powerful, uplifting and energising. Music is a spiritual thing.

The following affirmation or cognitive thoughts are mandatory.

3X I have energy
3X I am energised
3X I am full of energy
3X I have energy from God
3X I am energised by God
3X I feel energy form God
3X I am being energised by God
3X I have energy from the superconscious
3X I am energised by the superconscious
3X I feel energy from the superconscious
3X I am being energised by the superconscious
3X I have energy from birds
3X I am energised by birds
3X I feel energy from birds
3X I am being energised by birds
3X I have energy from animals
3X I am energised by animals
3X I feel energised by animals
3X I am being energised by animals
3X I have energy from children
3X I am energised by children
3X I feel energy from children
3X I am being energised by children
3X I have energy from my clients
3X I am energised by my clients

3X I feel energy from my clients
3X I am being energised by my clients
3X I have energy from people
3X I am energised by people
3X I feel energy from people
3X I am being energised by people

Superconscious is a higher mind from which life comes. If your life is too hard you will need to work with the superconscious, I will explain the superconscious mind at later stages. Any thought, goal, ideal, plan, must come from the superconscious mind.

Affirmations or Cognitive thinking for where you are at the moment.

3X I am in an internal world, a psychological world where life and energy come from
3X I am in the inner world of mental and psychological well being
3X I am into privacy and freedom (my life and energy come from freedom and privacy).
3X Directional scoring conversation is destructive so let go
3X External world let go the world of surviving and ego let go
3X I am into the positive thinking I look for the good
3X I am into loving and warm thoughts
3X I am into spiritual, motivational and uplifting thoughts
3X I am on a path of living I enjoy my day
3X I am into things that I like, absorb and fascinate
3X I am into things which turn me on
3X I am into self-esteem how much I like myself
3X I like myself more today than yesterday and I like myself more tomorrow than today
3X I have people cooperation and support towards my role and mission.
3X I ask God to take care of me
3X I ask God to look after me
3X I ask God to give me the potency, the power, the will whatever is required to fulfil my role and mission

3X I ask the subconscious mind to give me the strength, the stamina, the potency, the energy, whatever is required to bring a more stable system

After this set of 'affirmations' I listen to music again and again. Then I have breakfast and take my tablets.

All the above affirmations have an effect on us and after a period of time you will be able to recite them by heart. But, for now we need to write them down and repeat them in front of the mirror until you will see the logic and follow them. The first set of 'affirmations' used during the morning are for happiness, for feeling good. Also, you believe something wonderful will happen to you, looking for something nice like a cheque in your mail, a friend will turn up at your door, etc. If you believe that something wonderful will happen, something nice will happen.

Second set of affirmations are for energy and for whereabouts you are at the moment. As I said you take place, and spend a lot of time in the internal world. What is also true is that the external world is full of ego and scoring points. Affirmation of privacy, as well as affirmations', of about things which turn me on and absorb me are relevant. The cognitive thinking is expanding to some degree around God and the superconscious mind, of which you will learn later.

The following set of 'affirmations', will be used to gain energy faster and recover faster.

They are good for 'standard' CFS as well as 'extreme chronic fatigue'.

3X I am angry
3X I feel angry
3X I have anger
3X I am entitled to anger
3X I have the right to anger
3X I have anger as a drive, I have anger as energy.

3X I am angry to get things done in front of apathy of others
3X I am angry to tell people they crossed the boundary
3X I am angry to stand up for my rights.

I am angry with selfish people, the worst thing is selfish. Giving is living. The more you give the more it is. Others do not have the opportunities you do. You keep the pool empty. Surviving, surviving.

I am angry with idiots. The same thing over and over again, You do not have a mind and brain use it. Picking on old people. Practising shields at 3 o'clock in the morning,

I am angry with knockers. One moment of fun knock, one moment of intelligence knock. One moment of emotions knock. Chest for everything, chest destroys everything.

I am angry with people who trample on peoples feelings. Trample on feelings trample on people. Bulldozer, bulldozer.

I am angry with people who do not take their education and make the contribution, So many things to do, so much to do. Shame on you, shame on humanity.

I am angry with people who would not give five minutes of their time. The guy is sick he/she needs your help.

The above statements use anger to uplift the spirit, and also to get energy. Apart from music and 'affirmations' which are always there, you will find yourself always using coffee, probably 5 small cups a day. It generates adrenalin and energy. You will also need to take multivitamins, because caffeine destroys vitamins and minerals. Do not drink coffee 6 hours before you go to bed, so you can fall asleep.

3X I am angry with my father
3X I feel angry with my father
3X I have the right to be anger with my father

In your life, especially now when you are very sick there must be a lot of people who could have helped you but for some reasons they turned their back on you. It can be a brother, sister, doctor, psychologist, mother, friends etc. In my case, I have people who turned their back on me like my sister, mother, father, psychologist, and another psychologist. With these people I always have anger because of the sort of things they have done to me. How they ignore me, how they hurt me etc. The anger we have we only use now, after it serves the purpose we discard the anger. We control the anger, as we are able to control all the negative emotions.

This is about my father. How dare you turn your back on me and you leave me out with doctors, nurses, chemists etc.?

You allow my mum to attack me with so much force, so much energy for a telephone number? You allow mum to attack me, to tell her that I feel good so you two can sleep.? My life is more important than your sleep.

You dominate and pick like a vulture, you attack me while under attack from my mother, my sister and my girlfriend.

You are a scavenger. You make such a fuss about 200 $, my life is more important than that. You feel guilty, you start doing a bit too hard.

You run away. You want me to run your life, and you can not do a basic thing. Make sure you are getting back form the universe to feel for people because you are a monster. Stay and watch with my mum and other people.

3X I am angry with my mum
3X I am entitled to anger with my mum
3X I have anger with my mum
3X I feel angry with my mum

How dare you turn your back on to me and you leave me out in the jungle with doctors, chemists, and nurses.? You have the money to get me out of here, yet you stay and watch.

You compare yourself to my cousin she is fifty. You compare yourself with my old time girlfriend who is in the past. Millionaires, millionaires idiots. You use so much vengeance, so much force to tell you that I feel good, so you can sleep. My life is more important than that.

You use so much force to get the telephone number from me. After 50 years of being together you sold me out to a guy you have just met. Nothing about him, he does all the shit jobs. Make sure you will be getting back from the universe. That is what fighting and control does.

3X I am angry with my sister
3X I feel angry with my sister
3X I am entitled to anger with my sister
3X I have the right to be angry with my sister.

How dare you attack me for 8 years, I have been sick for 8 years and you attack me continuously. Nothing about you, you have no social intelligence, you cannot dress. You do all the shit work. I have fought for you with the job, I fought for you for an apartment, for you were killing yourself, poor woman. They need you otherwise they drop you. I ask the universe to give it back to you because you are cold and a dog. You have never done anything for me.

3X I am angry with Psychologist 1
3X I am entitled to anger with Psychologist 1
3X I have the right to be angry with Psychologist 1

How dare you turn your back on to me and leave me in the jungle A guy who has been with you for one year, one year with Psychologist 2, and with the manager before you started, and could not be bothered. A guy who has been practising for 12 years and studied for 6 years should be a role model. You sell me out to women you just met. Make sure you get it back from the universe to your daughter to feel for people because you are a dog and selfish. Selfish, you take away my good points, put your negative on me, you sell me out to a woman you just met. You sell me out to the two guys from the reception. Make sure you are getting it back from the universe, to your daughter, to feel for people because you are cold and selfish.

3X I am angry with Psychologist 2.
3X I feel angry with Psychologist 2.
3X I have the right to feel angry with Psychologist 2.

How dare you turn the back on me twice. I have been with you for a year, always thinking about you, always supporting you, always there for you. Sitting on a chair we are going to do meditation, good for you. What did you say? For months she would not forget me. I pour my soul and heart out, still she would not forget. The game of dominance and power a builder, philosophy. You only gave me shit stuff, you send me to a community guy, to the group guys, to GROW, to shit jobs. Make sure you are getting back from the universe to your son to feel for people, cold woman.

Instead of the names I used, use names of the people who turn their back on you so you have plenty of energy and plenty of drive. These 'affirmations' can be used by people with extreme CFS as well as 'standard' chronic fatigue. Other cognitive thinking I use is for love and current situation.

4X Love is fifty percent of life
4X Love is a conquer of all problems.
4X Love is a builder of life
4X Love is the doorway which kicks open all the possibilities of the Universe
4X Love is a conquer of all problems
4X I am a loving, lovable and loved human being.
4X I have love
4X I am loved
4X I feel love
4X I have universal love
4X I open my arms and let universal love come to me.

4X I have love from God
4X I am loved by God.
4X I feel love from God
4X I am being loved by God.
4X I have love from the superconscious
4X I am loved by the superconscious
4X I feel love from the superconscious mind.
4X I am being loved by the superconscious
4X I have love from birds
4X I am loved by Birds.
4X I feel love from Birds.
4X I am being loved by Birds
4X I have love from animals
4 X I am loved by animals
4X I feel love from animals
4X I am being loved by animals
4X I have love from children
4X I am loved by children.
4X I feel love from children
4X I am being loved by children.
4X I have love from my clients
4X I am loved by my clients
4X I feel love from my clients
4X I am being loved by my clients.
4X I have love from people
4X I am loved by people
4X I feel love from people
4X I am being loved by people.
4X Slowly and surely I move forward with my life
4X I believe with confidence that I move forward with my life
4X I am free of danger, if there was danger the world would not exist
4X I am confident in all areas of my life
4X I am confident in my interaction with people
4X Until I get into the internal world with more stability it will be a
while so I will be patient

4X Until the drive of anger and hostility kicks in is going to be hard so I have patience

4X Using the emotions to imply is bad control. Nothing is bad thinking makes so (control the emotions, control the behaviour, control the individual)

4X I am good enough even if I have done something bad

A lot of material used for self-help groups might not have been proved scientifically but intuitively they work. Isolated by so long you will deal with a lot of situations and challenges. CFS is a situation. A situation is something you can handle. The word problem is negative and is hard for you to handle. CFS is not a challenge because it is too much to handle for a challenge. Throughout this situation you will encounter many challenges, situations and opportunities.

Some of the negative emotions encountered or areas which you need to work on in CFS/Me, are but not in order: Denial, Trigger thoughts, Inner rules and regulations, General Anxiety, Anxiety attacks, Social Anxiety, Anger, Performance anxiety, Panic Attacks, Depression, Obsessive and Compulsive thoughts, Paranoia, Supressed emotions (catharsis), Self-Esteem, Fear of failure, Fear of rejection, Unfinished business (jobs, relationships), Books in growing kids, your current relationships with your parents. I know you wanted to conquer chronic fatigue, otherwise you would not have read this book.

Psychologically ready

I am more referring to people with 'standard' CFS, you face the situation and would like to change, but there is a lack of motivation apart from the fact that you are sick. You need to be psychologically ready, you are ready to change the current situation and change the CFS. People who set themselves a goal at the beginning of the year do not achieve it because they are not psychologically ready. To be psychologically ready is to see the good points and dwell on them over and over. Also, the reasons to change will help you again by dwelling on them.

Medication

There are a lot of medications which come under anxiety/depression. There is SSRI the latest medication which means selective serotonin reuptake inhibitors. They work on a chemical in your brain which is called serotonin. They are preferred over other classes of antidepressants such as Tricyclic and MAO (monoamine oxidase inhibitors)

SSRI Generic Brand Names
Paroxetine (Aeropax)
Escitalopram (Lexapro)
Citalopram (Celexa)
Sertraline (Zoloft)
Fluvoxamine (Luvox)
Fluoxetine (Prozac)

Usually the above class of antidepressant cover your Cognitive thinking and it would be harder to work on in psychology. The only one which I recognize as helpful is Paroxetine, I have been with that for 20 years now, and never had a side effect problem and as I said it does not cover your cognitive thinking. I have to confess that I have only been on Aeropax and Lexapro. Good luck in trying the others,

There is a newer class of antidepressant which targets the neuro transmitter such as norepinephrine, in addition to serotonin.

Typical generic names are:
Bupropion
Duloxetine
Venlafaxin
Mirtazapine
Trazodong

I have tried Venlafaxine and Mirtazapine and both cover the cognitive thinking, making it impossible to work with a psychologist. Good luck in trying the rest. There are other form of medication called antipsychotic medications. Maybe you will be able to take them with the doctor or psychiatrist. They are also used as anti-anxiety medications. All antidepressants are also anti-anxiety medications. That is because at the root of any negative emotions lies fear.

2.0 Development

Change in the system

If your life does not require changes, in the sense that your system is travelling well and there is no need to change, do not change. The changes in your system might produce an unbalanced system where life might become hard. Live in the moment. By living in the moment I mean live your life one day at a time. There is no future, no past, only the moment. In this world you will find an abundance of two things, everyday moments and relationships. But relationships requires work, work on both sides of the relationship to keep it alive. The eastern philosopher introduces you to the idea of mindful meditation. Specifically where you live your life being aware of your surroundings and yourself which is at the moment. I suggest to let go of the past and let go of the future. You learn from the past and then you let go. It is with the past that you can do nothing but learn and let go. The process of letting go is a powerful tool in personal development. You will see the need to let go and then you let go. You let go from the gut E.g.: 'I let go of a relationship which is finished and it is in the past there is nothing I can do about it'. This can be applied to a lot of situations where you need to let go.

Once you live in the moment

you will start living. Living is in the moment because this is the only things abundant. In general people are negative and what they really remember about facts are negatives. They will dwell on a negative situation. If you make a habit of reliving the moments in a day, more than once you will have lots of living moments. This is one thing that you can try and if it works you can keep doing it.

Watch your energies

You will need energy to rewrite your system, to re-programme yourself. That is why I said you will need energies. Also, to be happy you need to charge the battery at a level of 70%. While you re-programme yourself, you will have more and more energy.

You will need to know where you lose energy, and where you gain energies. While in contact with some people you will lose energy, while in contact with others you will gain energies. Completing tasks will give you energies, not completing them will make you feel deflated and procrastinated.

Sleeping is important, proper sleep will get you energies. Bad sleep will lose energies. When you have a lot of energies it is possible to save them for later. We all have a battery in the subconscious mind where energies are used and stored. Save energy for later, by commanding 'I save energy in the subconscious mind'. Or release it by commanding saying: 'I release energy from my subconscious battery'.

Watching energies is a very important process. I have not watched my energies and ended up with Chronic Fatigue Syndrome, a very hard condition where you only have 12% of the battery capacity.

Make a living

If you would be an eastern philosopher master in India you would not have the need to make a living, you would be surrounded by people and making a living would not be necessary. But here in the western world you would need to make a living. You will need to provide for yourself and at the same time develop yourself. Do not expect that someone will give you a job. You will need to get a job and build jobs.

It is hard to make a living and I am referring to 'good jobs' which pay well, they are challenging and you get your social skills. If you do not focus on making a living the sheriff will get your furniture and you will end up on streets.

Know yourself

The reason I put this on the top of priority is because if you do not know yourself you will live in ignorance and confusion. Know what you are doing and why are you doing it. What makes you tick and what do you want from life.? These are the type of questions you need to ask yourself. Some authors put knowing yourself at the end of the development. I believe it is very important and you need special time in the beginning, not to live in Ignorance and Confusion.

Assume total responsibility

for your life. It is very important to be totally responsible. All your life you can not give total responsibility away. You are in charge of your life, you are the architect of your life. People in general are not doing things for you. So, if you want to progress in your life you need to be totally responsible, You can not be responsible in one area and not responsible in other areas. Totally responsibility is required. Personally I was not totally responsible, and I needed to start from the beginning everything again. You can not give away responsibility, only control. You need to become responsible yourself and let go of blaming. Blaming everyone for things you need to be responsible, blaming the government, blaming the doctors. Although the government should be responsible they are not and they probably do not care in a majority of cases.

So, stop blaming everyone apart from you. And if you blame yourself, you still do not do it, thinking there are no requirements for the action to take place. A good example would be my mum, who grew up in a negative destructive environment. When she does not have anyone else to blame, but herself, she lets go of the action. Blaming looks in the past 'who did it?', Where areas responsibility looks in the future 'what can we do from here?'. Being solution oriented rather than problems oriented, is good.

One high goal is the mission

It is believed that 4000 years ago, due to some proof, a movement to start changing the world started. It was decided that something must be done in order to change the current world of hurt, world of attack and world of security, Because life was so painful, a movement to change the world was started. Most of the knowledge to change the world was acquired 2000 years ago (not all but most). It does not make any sense to be born, multiply, work and die. There must be something more. And in my opinion we are all here for others. Great lovers such as Jesus of Nazareth, Buddha and Mohamed were born to teach the message of universal love and unite the world. They spoke of a world where everybody is united through love. These are the greatest lovers of our civilization. Others such as Mother Theresa, Albert Schweitzer and Florence Nightingale were also great. You only become great if you lose in a mission better and grander than yourself. I am not asking why greatness but how greatness. By loosing yourself in a mission which is grand, you change the world faster and you are also a role model for other people. 'Built to last' and 'From good to great' by Jim Collins who emphasizes how to look and become great. It is probably put in your soul before you were born. From good to great shows how to become great from good and that good is the enemy of the great, 'Built to last' emphasizes how to build institutions for the next century and well after. Achieving greatness means that you serve with honour the human race and is the reason that your time spent on earth is well worth.

Unfortunately only 2-5% of any given generation achieve their mission. If we all fulfilled our missions the world would have been better a long time ago. Significant contributions to change the world faster are to be proliferated. Thinking big, also changes the world faster and in the same time you are more fulfilled, because you have made significant contributions. You do not have to be a psychologist to understand that.

To achieve and know your mission to find out why are you here, is to always ask the question: 'What should it be?', 'What can it be?', 'How should it be?'. My current mission is to achieve significant contribution and make the world a better place. It can be in any area.

Peace of Mind

Why is peace of mind so important? If you do not have it you will not enjoy life in general. So, it is your duty to keep your mind clear. Your goal is to be free of mind clutter, so you can enjoy life and what you have. It is a very important goal in becoming a happy person. A happy person is who you would like to be. Eliminate all the problems of your mind which do not have any place. A way to peace of mind is to write down on a piece of paper what bothers you on one column and how to let go of them from your gut. As I previously mentioned your letting go is a powerful tool. You will develop a good habit of letting go.

Work with the superconscious mind

If you do not master the superconscious mind your life would be hard. By going with the flow in the right direction dictated by you, you will make life easier. The superconscious mind is a mind above all the other minds, of which we all have access at any time. All life comes from the superconscious mind. Once you have a superconscious solution it will be simpler and you will think 'Why didn't I think of it. It will answer all the questions. It will be full of energy and has a feeling of elation. The superconscious mind can be accessed through written goals, affirmations, day dreaming, relaxation etc. When you use the superconscious mind the solution will come and you need to take immediate action, otherwise it thinks you are not serious. So master the superconscious solution by taking the first step and then follow the steps as they come, Synchronicity is a process of using the superconscious mind, where 3 or more events relate to themselves to bring you a solution. Events which seemed not related to each other are connected in order to bring a solution. Serendipity is the process of making happy discovery on your way to your goal.

The superconscious mind has access to all data making the solution true or false. The more you use the superconscious mind the easier it becomes to use. You can get a lot of energy from the superconscious mind, sometimes running for days without sleep. Personally I forget to take action in order to start the superconscious solution and by doing that life becomes hard. You can activate the superconscious mind by going in solitude for 30 to 60 minutes. After which a solution will come up full of energy. You will need to take action and follow the steps of the solution.

Acquiring self-esteem

Self-esteem for me is the most important issue in the whole book. It is how much you love yourself, how much you like yourself, how much you accept yourself unconditionally for who you are. With self-esteem you can face and do anything, you can face rejection, you can face failure, you can face anything. It is important to acquire self-esteem and to become a generator of self-esteem. By the power of suggestion you will have some changes in your self-esteem towards the ego. But you will become hungry for self-esteem to keep away the ego suggestions. The affirmation area is powerful tool to programme your mind, and we use them to acquire self-esteem Affirmations are statements in the present tense, present tense because the subconscious mind only work in the present. Affirmation needs to be emotionalised and aloud for maximum input. They uses the word 'I' which can only be used by you. The subconscious mind does not take the negative 'not' e.g.: 'I am proficient' and 'I am not proficient'. You can replace not with regardless or without.

Because for years we used to 'hate' ourselves, it is hard to change overnight into 'love yourself'. We can love ourselves a bit more today than yesterday and a bit more tomorrow then today. Which can be transformed into following affirmations:

> 'I like myself more today than yesterday
> And 'I like myself more tomorrow then today'
> 'I like myself unconditionally'

Now on top of this affirmation you need to like yourselves in various roles, e.g.: Good father. See yourself as a good father, spend quality time with your child, love your child. I love my son, And you should use any roles you have such as; teacher, employee, husband and so on.

After re-living these roles and using affirmations you will feel the difference in 3 weeks, a month, 3 months, a year and 3 years. To acquire self-esteem it takes on average of 3 to 4 years. After that you will be able to go anywhere, because you love yourself. So use the following affirmations aloud:

4X I like myself unconditionally
4X I like myself more today than yesterday
4X I like myself more tomorrow than today
4X I am a worthy and valuable human being no matter what I do and say (or regardless of what I do and say I am still a worthy and valuable human being')
4X I am a worthy and valuable human being no matter what happens
4X I am good enough regardless how I go in any situation

4X I am good enough regardless how I do in any situation

4X I am good enough regardless what people think about me

4X I am good enough regardless what people say about me

4X I am good enough regardless of the people's opinion about me

4X I am good enough because GOD say so. He makes all people worthy and valuable with a mission on earth

4X I am good enough because I am the father of all children.

4X I am good enough because I am a good father, I love my child, I do the best thing for my child

4X I am good enough because I still have a relationship with my parents (others throw them in asylums and nursing homes).

4X I am good enough because I am committed to people

4X I am good enough because I am a sensitive person

4X I am good enough because I am a caring person

4X I am good enough because I am a doer and I complete actions

4X I am good enough because I do the best I can with the knowledge at the time.

4X I am good enough regardless of my mistakes\

4X I am a worthy and valuable human being regardless of my mistakes

Some of the affirmations are long and they become Cognitive thoughts. I am able to remember the affirmations by heart, because I have been doing them for a while. You are better off writing them down on a piece of paper. The subconscious mind is open to suggestions in the morning when you wake up and in the evening before you go to bed. If you are in an environment of rejection, I suggest that you repeat the affirmations/cognitive thoughts so you counter act the negative suggestion. Something else I need to mention is to leave some parts of yourself to the ego, around 20%. That is because it is a world of ego with scoring points and opinions about people. Also, you do not want to be used as a doormat that is where ego helps. In general, the ego takes the back seat of the car.

You may acquire self-esteem with your own affirmations. Even if you have self-esteem is good to repeat the affirmations from time to time because of the power of suggestion from being surrounded by a negative environment.

Fill your own mind with loving thoughts

On TV you get a lot of crimes and actions in the movies. Shows like news are negative in the sense that they emphasize the negative and not the positive. Wherever you go you will be surrounded by society's negativity. You will need to fill up your mind with spiritual, uplifting, loving, warm and positive thoughts. You can spend like 30 minutes per day of your time to focus on these positive thoughts. If it is not possible do it just once per week.

Learn to forgive

If this is the first personal development book discovered you will probably be upset with your parents, that is because they have not been supportive while you grew up. And you are entitled to be so. After a while you will need to forgive them. They did their best they could with the knowledge from their parents and so on. It is healthy to forgive and let go. Be selfish and let go of the past from the people who did wrong to you. Forgive but don't forget.

Take care of your body

The body is complicated and can perform a lot of functions in little time. It is known as the mind of the universe because it can do so many things including listening to the universe. It is also the temple of the soul. Take care of your body by giving it good food and good exercise. The diet is more important than exercise, 20% is exercise and 80% is diet. Ideally speaking of diet and books 30% of populations are obese and overweight. Thanks God that there are solutions for big problems that society has. Gary Taubes in his book 'Why you get fat and what to do about it', covers all the questions pertaining to weight loss. It is based on the research done at the end of 19th century and the beginning of 20th century, research forgotten. It also throws away the false believe we had from the research done at the end of 20th century. It is shown we should not eat to burn sugar and we should eat to burn fat. By burning sugar we create fat. By eliminating most of the starches (even all) and sugars for two weeks we set up the system to burn fat. And then once or twice a week we eat sugars and starches so the hormones leptin and testosterone can grow to eat the fat. You will also get rid of the craving of sugar and starches by cheating twice. They are called cheat meals because you do not eat meat and vegetables (as much as you want) and a bit of fruit (not too much because they contain fructose which is a sugar). A sugar is still sugar even if is natural. You will be able to stay without food for days. Until the hunt of animals was completed. And the fruits eaten at the time were small with little sugar. If you eat too much fruit you will not lose weight. It seems to me that this diet is the answer to society's problems and not portion control so much used these days, where you end up putting weight back on eating whatever you want.

World of love

Some people believe that there is a world of dominance. Is it? Some people who love power say there is a world of power. A world where people would push people around. The truth is that the world is a world of love. Derived from the movement in the superconscious of security where we would live to feel safe and secured. Love does that. The truth is the game of dominance, force fear and intimidation is boring. A game where you impose yourself on other people, could be this called living.? In order to change the world we need to bring into the world what was meant to be and that is the world of love and after that change it. The jump to a new world as tried by some people is too much to ask. We need first to unite ourselves in love, and after that, change it so there is no hurt. You can be like a flower where energies are flowing through you. You have children so to have loving relationships. You have marriages to have loving relationships. You only need to give a bit of love away so there would be some coming back. The more you give, the more would come back. By following the steps in this book you will become a loving person and a loving person is the one you should become. Just because is simple does not mean it is easy, this requires a lot of effort and the final outcome is worth waiting.

Deal with negative emotions

When I talk about negative emotions I do not talk about the emotions of loss of a relationship or the passing away of somebody you love. But about negative emotions such as doubt, fear, envy, resentment, guilt which are not warranted, and you spend a lot of time of dwelling on them and that stop you from achieving a happy fulfilled life. Justifications keep the negative emotions alive it cultivates them. You are saying 'I am entitled to this emotion ', or you say 'After so much trouble can I give up?' The idea is to let go of the luggage of negative emotions, get rid of them. Justification keeps the negative emotions alive. By dis-identifying you keep the emotions at bay, they lose control over you. 'I have anger but I am not the anger', 'I have anger but the anger is not me'. You are still here and the emotions will pass. Blaming is at the root of negative emotions. Once you stop blaming so the negative emotions stop. Negative emotions are learned throughout your life. Being judgemental is another way of keeping the negative emotions intact. Where there is a division there is a struggle. Responsibility and freedom go hand in hand. You obtain freedom to the degree to which you are responsible. As I previously mentioned the idea is to leave negative emotions like garbage and go ahead and fulfil your life. The difference between successful and non-successful people is how they deal with negative emotions, so they have time to have a happy fulfilled life.

Lack of childhood love affects the negative emotions. Parents must love themselves and from there, each other and the child.

General Anxiety

The main theme in general anxiety is worries. Apart from that there is always an impending sense of danger, you are not the beneficiary of life. Everything seems to be danger, the world is a danger, humanity is at danger, life is a danger. When you suffer from anxiety you will always be negative looking for the bad in everything.

Trigger thoughts or precipitating thoughts as called by psychologists are the thoughts before the emotion which triggers the event. They can be found after the event as well and they can be relieved through imagination. In anger example: 'How dare she says that to me.' In case of a relationship a sense of loss 'She does not love me anymore' when the relationship is finished. You need to stop yourself from identifying with your thoughts e.g. 'that is how relationships end'. 'There is nothing I can do to get him'. This is writing more appropriate trigger thoughts. You will need identifying rule which give rise to the trigger thoughts, because if not they will make you to hold on to them. You will need to look at concepts such as: 'guilt', 'anger', 'power', 'religion', 'love', 'uniqueness' etc. You will need to identify the trigger thoughts which rob you of living a fulfilling life. We need to replace them with more appropriate trigger thoughts. The trigger thoughts have a control over us.

After all, we cover so far, in general anxiety worries are the main theme. I recommend you the course run by. The Center for Clinical Studies. Is a very practical course in a sense that there are a lot of exercises and is also free. There is a worry diary where to stressful situations a series of logical questions are applied that thus deal with the worry. It is called the worry diary.

About the worries
What am I worried about? List my worry thoughts?
What am I predicting? How much do I believe it will happen? (0-100%)
What emotions am I feeling? And rate the intension of the emotion (0-100%)

Challenging the worry
What is the evidence for your predictions?
What is the evidence against my prediction?
How likely is it that I am predicting will happen? (0-100%)
What is the worst that could happen?
What is the best that could happen?
What is the mostly thing that will happen?
How helpful is for me to worry about this?
If the worst thing will happen what could I do to cope?
How else can I view the situation?
Balanced thinking
A more balanced and helpful thought to replace my worries is-------
How much do I believe in my predictions? (0-100%)
How intense are my feelings/emotions? (0-100%)

By challenging the worries they will have a less effect on to you to a point where they do not affect you.

Another way to deal with worries is to let go from the gut. E.g. Worried that you are going to fall in the shower even if you have taken all precautions not to fall. The trigger thoughts 'Hi what am I going to do?' I am going to fall. The anxiety that I am going to fall in the shower is not a truth, not a fact, not a reality just an unhelpful thought.

Letting go is like a deviation of energy, you do not stop it, you deviate it. How you need to let go, is practise. The more you are doing it the easier it will come. Do it for three times and the worry will disappear. We also need to practice mindful meditation which is in the present. In the present there is no fear e.g.: I rest my leg on the chair, My fingers touch my body, The corner of the table is there. And so on. Remember that worries are good to plan for the future.

Depression

There are two types of depression, one is reactive depression, where there are links to external events and endogenous which seems to come with no reasons. The reason I cover depression is that there is no reason to live for a lot of people, people try to take their own lives and we cannot watch how people suffering.

Depression is a continuous feeling of sadness from which it is hard to escape. In depression there is always a feeling of loss which triggers off the event. In order to deal with depression, we need to identify a feeling of loss and rob it of its powers. It maybe a feeling that we lost a childhood, that we do not have kids, that we wasted our life. In depression you need to identify what you lost and then replace them with more appropriate thoughts to today's life. If you do not have kids, you can sponsor some, there are so many kids without parents in this world. If you did not have a childhood try to live your inner child in the present.

When you wake up in the morning, the depression is at its peak. It is important not to identify with the feelings at these stage. You have a thought but you are not the thought, you have thought but the thought is not you, and you keep it at a distance (the thought comes and goes you are still here). You have a feeling but you are not the feeling, you have a feeling but the feeling is not you (they come and go and you are still here). As previously mentioned, there are trigger thoughts associated with the event. We have trigger thoughts such as;' What is the use of waking up?', 'I cannot face the day'. No matter what the thoughts and feelings are you need to get up and start your day.

Start with activities which will preoccupy the mind so to get out of the state of depression. Do not do an activity which does not serve the purpose of putting the mind on something else than depression. Every time you finish a task you will acquire energy and the more tasks you finish, the more energy you will have and that will get you out of depression.

We need to get out of bed to make sure the trigger thoughts of depression do not have time to trigger the depression, and also complete tasks which will energise you. Also seeking out beautiful surroundings, the sun, the nature, the light will ensure that you gradually snap out of the depression. The trigger thought identified has to be replaced by more helpful appropriate thoughts 'It is only the depression, it will pass', 'I do not have energy for anything', 'Slowly and surely I can build my energy'.

The hypnopompic state is a state between sleeping and waking up, as we return to consciousness. It plays an important part in influencing our waking up feelings. Before we go to bed we can say affirmations, positive cognitive thoughts for the morning. E.g.: 'I wake up in the morning feeling good.', 'I wake up in the morning tomorrow and I feel wonderful'. Do not make the affirmations too long that will confuse the mind. Also do not make it unbelievable: 'I wake up in the morning feeling fantastic'. The mind will not believe it. By dealing with depression you will empower yourself with the future knowledge of getting out of depression. So depression is not bad it is empowering. There will be definitely other chances of depression which you will know how to deal with. You will need to be patient and ready for setbacks but your perseverance will pay off in the end. As mentioned with trigger thoughts you will need to look at inner rules, regulations and distorted thinking which give rise to trigger thoughts and events. E.g.: Something is lost and there is nothing left of value in people's lives. That life without marriage is not worth living. There are a lot of things to do in your life as opposed to what you cannot do. It is believed that in depression, influenced by it, self-esteem is the culprit. Acquire self-esteem by seeing yourself as a worthy and valuable human being unconditionally or for who you are and not for what others think about you. By replacing inner rules, regulation and distorted thinking with more appropriate ones, the trigger thoughts, which give rise to depression will be dropped and replaced by more appropriate ones.

Anxiety attacks

Like in many forms of anxiety, at the base of anxiety lies fear. Fear is produced by being overwhelmed by actions and tasks. While suffering anxiety attacks, you will have numerous trigger thoughts, more than general anxiety. Some will be hard to stop. When they are not stopped, the adrenalin and fear will eat your body. In this period of time you will lose an enormous amount of body weight. Personally I lost 15 kilos in 3 days, because I could not stop the anxiety attacks. After 3 days of anxiety, the attacks stopped and realised that it was taking place in the spirit and not the mind. Doctor uses Valium to stop anxiety attacks, but sometimes it works and sometimes it does not work. You should not have more than 4 major tasks to work on, and also a small number of activities. If you have more than 4 tasks you will trigger anxiety attacks. If you have less than two you will not be able to work with the superconscious mind and life will be hard. You will always think about the one goal which will block the action from the superconscious mind. To get rid of the actions and tasks you will write them on paper. Actions on the left side and what to do about them on the right side. The letting go technique will come in handy and you know it by now. Let go of what you do not need e.g.:' I let go of building the house'

It can happen that this time the fear entered the gut, and you need to work on your gut. You need to replace trigger thoughts in your spirit. The trigger thoughts in your mind need to be replaced by more appropriate thoughts 'It is only temporary it will pass', 'Hi, what am I going to do?', 'Everything is OK I can handle the situation'. Working on the number of tasks and actions you do, combined with trigger thoughts will help you with anxiety attacks. You will need to work on the central theme of anxiety, which is worries.

Panic attacks

The reason you get panic attacks is because you lack fulfilment in your life. And I do not mean being busy, but meaningful tasks that fill your void in your life. Like relationships, meaningful purpose of life, goals which are important and so on. Panic attacks are anxiety, but in acute form. Trigger thoughts of panic attacks have a sense of urgency 'This is my death warrant', I am going to die', This is it'. I know panic attacks first hand, because I used to have them. Panic attacks start in elevators, in overcrowded places, and if you are by yourself in situations you do not like. In the middle of panic attacks your breath is short and you are panting. It is nothing to worry about, you are not going to die.

The trigger thoughts in panic attack need to be replaced by more appropriate and realistic ones. 'This is temporary, it will pass', 'this is the panic attack it will pass'. 'this is OK I can handle the situation'.

The trigger thoughts encountered in panic attacks will produce additional trigger thoughts such as 'I am going to have a heart attack', I am going to die', I am going to wet myself'. Trigger thoughts give rise to more trigger thoughts because of the physical symptoms they produce and so on. The key is not to identify with them, they are temporary, they will pass. You have a thought but the thought is not you. I have a thought, but I am not the thought. There is the mistaken inner view that if something bad can happen, something bad will happen. Such a belief is good in children, but not for a mature individual. If something bad can happen, in most occasions it will not happen. It is temporary, it will pass, is a positive way of looking at the trigger thought.

Paranoia

Recently I have discovered a patient with paranoia and because of that I will try to make a point about paranoia. Also you might think it is not a hard condition it can really have an effect on you. People will have paranoia so friends and other people will agree with them and give their self-esteem a boost. Every time you are right your self-esteem goes up. That is the whole mechanism of paranoia. Is also a feeling that everybody is gaining against you. There is strong evidence that the conclusion is not valid, but the person with paranoia will not agree. The trigger thoughts of people with paranoia are: 'They know I am right but they would not admit it', 'It is bloody unfair'. Until we understand why we always need to feel right it is very hard to get rid of paranoia.

Phobias

Phobia is a powerful fear which comes with an element of irrationality. We all have phobias. Some phobias are: fear of heights, fear of enclosed spaces, fear of spiders, fear of dentist (as I used to have), fear of public speaking, fear of dogs and so on. Just because you have a phobia does not mean that you have more anxiety than the general public.

Psychologists call phobias fixation phobias and traumatic phobias. The fixation phobia is the phobia which has not been outgrown (keeps us fixated) and keeps us at the same age. The traumatic phobia is connected with a single traumatic event which we did not understood fully. E.g.: Fear of fire, fear of public peaking, fear of dogs, fear of spiders. Whatever the phobia type is, it spells terrifying threats and has to do with the fear of losing control. The dentist will take control over our mouth and inflict pain. The dog is going to take us by the throat. There are many things over which we do not have control and we do no phobias, We can discuss the treatment with the dentist to give us drugs to anaesthetize. We can use a device which will keep the dog away. And slowly, slowly learn the art of public speaking, Flying is more safe than busses and trains, so the fall of the plane is highly unlikely.

The regulations, inner rules and distorted thinking can be used together with trigger thoughts to deal with phobias. We have nothing to fear from close paces, heights, fear of flying, fear of open spaces etc., provided we take up precautions which are good for everybody else.

Obsessive and compulsive thoughts

I could not believe that the condition of obsessive and compulsive thoughts could inflict such pain. Until I encountered people suffering and being on medication. As with previous kinds of anxiety, we need to look at the distorted thinking, inner rules and regulations and trigger thoughts and replace them with more appropriate thoughts for today's world and more mature views. As the name suggests the compulsive thoughts are those thoughts which compel us to perform certain unwanted actions and obsessive thoughts are those we see for what they are but refuse to go away. Examples of compulsive thoughts wash our hands even if they are not dirty, check the garage it is locked even if we checked it before. Obsessive thoughts are the thoughts that we have to please 'mummy' and 'daddy'.

If they wash and scrub everything that is associated with dirt, they will be a worthy and valuable human being. The trigger thoughts which accompany the obsessional feeling of cleanliness are: 'It will make me dirty and therefore repulsive', 'I will catch a terrible disease. 'I should never be able to get clean'.

When obsessive thoughts lead to compulsive ones, the trigger thoughts are possible 'It is the only way to stop the thought'. 'If I can only do that things will be OK' The trigger thoughts can be replaced by 'dirt easily washes off', 'things like that make no difference in life'. The rule is that you are a worthy and valuable human being because of who you are, and you are not worthy because somebody else says so even if it is somebody in authority. We have obsessive and compulsive thoughts to atone for a feeling of not being good enough. This is a rule which needs to be replaced. Another rule is that if you touch everything twice it will make it right or make one happy.

The trigger thoughts:' I will never be forgiven', 'How could I have done such thing', 'I must be a terrible person'. Give rise to the inner rule that you are the only person in the world that could do such things, that nobody will love you and that there is nothing you can do to be a worthy and valuable human being. Where the trigger thought is an obsessional one leading to a compulsive urge to do something dreadful is 'What is the worst possible thing I can do steal from somebody', 'kill somebody' it destroys all irrational thoughts. The trigger thought is the fear of your own bad imagination put there by an experience which punish 'badness' with feelings of guilt. When you endlessly check things, the trigger thought is 'What is one thing for the moment that will spoil my happiness'. No matter how sure you are, you still check things twice and sometimes do not know how to stop it. You must observe it and will eventually go. Do not be judgemental just observant. Even if you have compulsive and obsessive thoughts you have nothing to regret. You still deserve happiness and success in this life. The suffering of the people with obsessive and compulsive behaviour comes from the wrong interpretation with which these actions have been surrounded.

Conversion disorders and amnesia

In extreme cases they are rare. I put a chapter on this because I know of people who suffer from amnesia and conversion disorders and I have encountered myself in terms of mind shutting down. Also I lost my hearing which is a conversion disorder.

The trigger thoughts involved in conversion disorders are: 'I cannot handle this',' I must blot out everything.' And in a major form of conversion disorder the person collapses (like my mother did). Another trigger thought is ', 'If I am sick, people will leave me alone'. This trigger thought is carried on from childhood where you could get away with being sick. No we are not in childhood anymore, when an adult will take care of us when we have too much to handle. We need to apply mature rules and regulations to the current situation. If it is too much, let go of some them, tell your self that you can handle the situation, and all the physical functions begin to return to normal.

The power of positive thinking

Thinking has power and is best described by positive thinking. I do not want to omit the negative emotions which are part of us. By focusing on positive you will attract positive and by focusing on negative you will attract negative in your life. By focusing on positive you will be mentally healthy. By having a habit of focusing on negative you will not have good mental health. By negative emotions I mean worry, anxiety, fear, anger which is not related to losing someone or divorcing. Instead of focusing on negatives you will focus on your goals and have no time for the negatives.

Change need to like or want. If you look properly need, the dependency is applied too often in our lives. More appropriate would be to replace them by 'like' and 'want'. There are things we need but not so many as we tell to ourselves.

Change 'awful' to 'inconvenienced'. Awful means something bad happened. Inconvenient is a word which causes just a bit of nuisance. To deal with awful we use contingency plan that things are not going to go the way we want to: trains will run late, people will let you down, jobs will take longer. We need to recognize life for what it is, not for what we want it to be. Saying the word awful is also judgemental and keeps the negative emotions alive, something we do not want.

Change 'must' or 'should' to 'could'. It is important to re-examine values, actions and beliefs, sometimes because they were put in us by some other people. 'Must' and 'should' brings a sense of duty but 'could' brings an element of choice which we need.

Change 'judge' and 'evaluate' to 'observe.' By being judgemental you keep the negative emotions alive, and by observing them you use the highest form of intelligence assigned to the human race. Evaluating is unavoidable like values. We do not obtain values if you are not evaluating. Reserving judgements until there is more data is a way to behave.

Change 'hurt' to 'teach'. We have to recognize that we often learn more from the people who want to hurt us, then people who are nice. To allow to be hurt is to allow the person with intent to achieve his purpose. But it also gives us the opportunity to look at ourselves; ready to take offence; unrealistic expectations; that others will not treat us the way we want to.

Change 'embarrass' to 'amuse'. Embarrassment is a fear that we would be laughed at. As to be seen as a buffoon is not what we want, an incompetent person that is. You would not like your self-imaging to beat the mercy of someone else's. Embarrassment is a fear which enters life around 4 to 5 years. Also the more embarrassed we feel, the more we invite others to laugh. And the more we can laugh at ourselves the less we are going to be laughed at. So change 'embarrass' to 'amuse' and see the joke with everybody else.

Change 'scare' to 'confront'. One way in dealing with fear is to confront the fear. By confronting the fear we see things different and you are not paralysed by fear. Life is not a secure business. By facing the fear we learn from that and we develop our human potential.

Change 'discourage' to 'challenge'. Discouraged means doing things has gone out of you. A way of dealing with discourage is to change it to 'challenge'. Challenge is uplifting and generates its own energy. Challenge is something you rise to.

More about the power of thinking and the power of words

People who have a psychological problem use words such as: 'awful', 'bad', 'hurt', 'embarrass', etc. They also use evaluation and judgement in their daily life. Life is seen as intimidating, overwhelming and dangerous and have a vocabulary of incompetence and failure. You can compare these messages about yourself with messages sent by someone who sends deprecating comments all the time. You will feel inadequate, a failure, low in confidence that you do not amount to much.

About the power of words. If we want to change psychologically we need to use the right words. Words have power and you begin to recognize this by covering this book. Words are symbols which represent reality. The power of suggestion for example when you say to yourself that you are stupid a lot of times, you will believe you are stupid.

If you believe that you are worthy and valuable, and you tell that to yourself numerous times you believe you are worthy. The verb 'to be' or 'I am', is the verb which helps us in viewing the power of words. 'I am tired', 'I am depressed', 'I am worried', 'I am helpless'. They represent me temporarily and not me permanently. A more appropriate word would be; 'I feel depressed', 'I feel sad', 'I feel helpless'. Other areas to consider in the power of words are the adjectives. E.g.: 'stupid', 'idiot'. Use adverbs and see the difference. He acted stupidly, He acted like an idiot. This is the difference between actions and labels. Actions are temporary and labels are permanent.

Avoid distorted thinking like; **Overgeneralisation.** For one wrong event you make it General. This is overgeneralisation failing a test in mathematics, makes me a bad mathematics student.

Personalization. When things have nothing to do with us but in our imagination would be directed at us. She did not turn up for the meeting because she was sick, and he believes that the reason she did not turn up is because she does not like him.

False conclusions. By basing the conclusion of an isolated events fails the test, I will fail the whole subject. Or by basing the conclusion on no event at all, failing one subject and I will fail the whole course.

Exaggeration and magnification. This is the process where minor events are seen as major importance. She forgets his birthday and he accuses her of not loving him. Obviously he does not understand what love is.

Polarized thinking. It is a tendency to ignore the middle **ground,** things are either black or white, not grey. The compromise is discarded and the debate does not take place.

Avoid comparisons. We obtain useful information through comparisons. But when it becomes a habit and involves evaluations they are unnecessary. Our old friend the self-esteem, is the culprit again and is too low. It was not as good as the last time. It was not as good as George. There should be individual satisfactions following the performance and accurate assessment of the performance. This comparison stays in the way of the full understanding of one's own capabilities. You can not be as good as 'X' because you are different, you have different life experiences, different opportunities, different upbringing and you should be as good as you.

In another simplistic way at looking at distorted thinking as comparisons, that you always compare your ego with another ego, the opinions of other people to your performance. Like comparing Segovia with BB King, they are both masters, who is to say that one is better than the other one.? Working on distorted thinking and false comparisons and trigger thoughts we can now work on other general problem such as lack of assertiveness, inability to be open, selfishness, difficulty in accepting others. **Selfishness** this is my top of the parade of problem.

The trigger thoughts associated with selfishness are: 'I must hang on to what is mine', 'Other people do not give anything to me', 'If I give things I will regret it afterwards', 'Giving involves losing never living', 'If someone has less than me it is their fault', 'If everybody works as hard as me, they would not need anything from me'. Such a life does not contain the understanding that giving has own rewards. That the more you give the more there is to go around. Some people are low on their luck. People are not equal at birth in terms of opportunities, and teaching, to base their lives.

Difficulty in accepting others. Why others are not like I want them to be. This is the main topic of people who have difficulty in accepting others. Nobody has the right to dictate to others what they should think and feel. If everybody wanted people to be the same, it would be boring and also a recipe for disaster.

Inability to open. These four problems, lack of assertion, inability to open, selfishness, difficulty in accepting others are part of the social intelligence, one of the most important intelligence, your ability to get on well with others, your ability to blend with others. As mentioned before, 85% of success comes from happy involvement with other people. People who do not open up about themselves have the following trigger thoughts: 'No one is interested in hearing about me'. Telling other people my real thoughts give them power over me'. 'If people knew what I am really like I will lose their friendship', For some showing your feelings is a sign of weakness.

Lack of assertion. Trigger thoughts of people who lack in assertion are: 'I will make him angry with me', 'I shall look silly'; 'I will always end up tongue tied if I try to speak up for myself', These trigger thoughts arise from early childhood we have rights to stand up for ourselves. That we must do what they like without answering back. The inner rules needs to be replaced by a more appropriate ones. Standing up for your rights is good for everybody. We shall be weary of over assertive people. By asserting ourselves, bit by bit, we will manage to fully assert ourselves.

Anger like fear it was put there by mother nature. In order to assert yourself over people who trample over you. It was put there to stand up for our rights, or to tell people they crossed the boundary. Anger is an expression of fear, of anxiety. In today's society anger is not accepted e.g. angry with your boss, angry with your parents. Anger poison the system and needs to be taken out. Anger is associated with fight and fear with flight. What gives rise to anger is a threat which can be real or imaginary. Threats can be to our authority, property, security, and so on. Anger, when used verbally can have an effect on relationships, it can upset people, he/she can discard the respect etc. Anger depends on the habit of blaming, As I said, anger poisons the system, and we need to deal with this. With your kicks you can get rid of anger, with shout you can express your anger, with your hands you can kick, and with your teeth you can bite. This is how you deal with anger which cannot be expressed due to society's requirements. Some trigger thoughts of anger are:' How dare she/he says that to me', 'How dare she is trying to get what is mine'. 'How dare you do that, I am going to get you.' The best way to deal with anger is to recognize the distorted inner thinking and regulations which give rise to anger and to work on trigger thoughts. Self-control is something else you can use. You are entitled to anger with your boss, but you can not express it, you need a frustration bag. So, you will need to work with anger. Stress that is externally orientated that forces you to do something that is not good. But stress which is goal oriented is positive and gives you vitality.

Confronting

In order to change you need desire. How badly do you want it. But to change things you need to face them. For any change you will pay the price, the later the change the bigger the price. This is the philosophy of reality, to change yourself where ever you are at the moment. Confronting is healthier than evasion.

Relationships

The most important relationship in your life is the relationship with your parents. It outlasts businesses, careers, marriages. It lasts until passing away. How to grow happy, vibrant, healthy, and loving kids? That comes down to the most important aspects of growing kids and this is self-esteem in children. The role of parents is to generate self-esteem in children. If you do not do that you will fail in your parenthood. You will need to make self-responsible and self-reliant children, who will make other people life's wonderful. They will also make a contribution in their life. They will handle whatever life throws at them. Parents make mistakes, they are allowed to make mistakes, but the main principle in growing children is to give self-esteem to children. They do not belong to us, they are not here to posses, they are here to be nurtured. Principles you need to use when growing children: Do not use destructive criticism. It passes straight into the subconscious mind becoming the truth.

Children need love. You show children your life by looking in the eyes and say 'I love you no matter what you do. I love you unconditionally'. The children need to know the word of love.

Parents are like Gods to children. And children need approval and love in order to grow. Parents need to be supportive, loving and kind. Children need gentleness and praise. Tell them you love them every day, so they know they are loved. If you do not know how to love they will teach you. Things you need to teach children:

Love them unconditionally whatever they do, love them
Eye contact to show your love
Hug and embrace the child as physical contact.

Focus attention on your child. Spend time every day with your child and tell them they are valuable. Believe in your child and tell him that. Allow the valued opinion of your child Teach the children to love themselves and say over and over 'I like myself', in front of the mirror. Children grown this way are popular, they get along very well with others and have better grades. To grow children you will need to get the ego out of the way. It is possible to apologize to your children to undo the past. Children who have been apologised to by their parents will be transformed overnight. Apologise to your children for the destructive criticism used throughout their lives. Promise not to do it again and allow them to remind you if you use it. Is this destructive criticism? and say' yes I apologise'.

I have come from a destructive negative environment and hope that this chapter will help people in growing wonderful children.

Mature relationship in the family

While growing up the parents are the main social context for our lives. Reaching the age of a teenager, the siblings take over this social relationship and do not love their parents too much. Once you reach the age of maturity the relationship with parents comes back and in its place a mature relationship take place. The family, parents and siblings together with children and partners provides the support to grow emotionally and psychologically. As previously said the relationship between you and your parents is a mature relationship and it has the following attributes:

Understanding. As a personal opinion the parents are here to nurture and support even in advanced years. So, a sense of understanding of what are we doing by them is important. Otherwise we will change our career and relationship towards something they like.

Space means freedom from your parents. It means that your parents do not try to interfere with your life. It also means they are not trying to live their lives through you.

Equality. The game of dominance does not have a place in equality. Equality is like a partnership, Parents are not parents anymore, they are your equal.

Support means parents will support and help when you need without too much questioning.

Guilt. A constant punishment that we have done something wrong. Guilt is used by parents to control us while growing up. But it can be used also at later stages in lives. If you have done something to feel guilty about then deal with it by atoning or asking God for forgiveness. But when parents are trying to make you feel guilty go on and refuse to give in to guilt.

Love. The expression of love even in maturity is beneficial to both sides. While we grew up with the withdrawal of love, it should not be so in the later stage of the relationship.

Health and strength. A parent with low health and strength will affect us in our relationship with them, no matter how much we want to help. If they give away the control in what should be done to them, this will help and make the situation more bearable, because we will have some control over our lives

Enjoyment. In our teenage years our parents no longer provide us with joy and fulfilment. The pears take the place. This process is part of the growing process where we do not love our parents that much. As previously mentioned this growing up relation is replaced by a more mature one. I know that in these times the parents use guilt to control us and put us down. Maybe it is a sign of not being very close to them.

Acceptance. Also at this moment I do not depend on my parents' approval of me, except for years ago when I was dependent on them. Many people are still depending on the opinion of their parents about them, that they have to prove themselves to their parents that his mum has an image of the manhood that the son needs to be, that the father has an image of what kind of women his daughter needs to be.

Openness. Open means that you can be honest with your parents about everything. You can refuse, you can disagree with them. The degree of security you enjoy in your relationship is how open you can be with them. If you are not open, you might not be accepted by them and they will withdraw their love from you.

More on Relationships

I would like to spend a little time on relationships because apart from the moment, this is the most abundant thing in life. I would also use relationships as the basis of your emotional life. Major problems in relationships is compatibility. You and the other person are not compatible. It happens more when you are in your twenties. There is nobody at fault it just happens. If incompatibility will happen you need to move on and look for someone else more compatible on your road in finding your ideal person. Despite incompatibility people still stay in relationships. They do that because of what other people might think about them. You are the person who cares most about your relationship. Relationships are successful if: similarly attracts in all areas sex, money, children, spare time. Opposites attract in the areas of temperament. An extrovert is compatible with an introvert person. A 50% extrovert is compatible with a 50% introvert. So, there is no clash in the time the two people talk. Commitment: 100% commitment is required. You do not get out of the relationship. Similarly happy people attract. Do not enter in a relationship where someone is unhappy believing that you can change the other person. People do not change until they follow some things from this book. Liking and respect: is required in a relationship. Infatuation is not enough to keep relationships alive. Communication: You need communication, back and forward. Without communication a relationship dies. You need quantity and quality of communication. Also speaking and listening. Why relationships do not work: Trying to change the other person. As I mentioned before what you see is what you get. People do not change unless they do some of the things from this book. Jealousy nothing to do with the other person but to do with you, you do not feel you are lovable. Say over and over again 'I am a loving, lovable and loved human being'. 'I like myself unconditionally', I love myself'. Self-pity, feeling sorry about yourself that you cannot cope say 'I can cope' and get busy. Lack of commitment you only commit yourself as much as the other person does. It is a trading relationship, you need to be fully committed. Amongst other things life is a journey, a journey where you can find the compatible person in your life. Isn't good that the relationships did not work? Because I could not find this one. If you want to shorten the waiting time for an ideal relationship you will need to write on a piece of paper, a left column with the good points of the person you want to get and a right column of the bed points of the other person you do not want to have. You will find the person with good points, but they will have bad points as well. After this go and find him or her at the appropriate places. Do not go to the pub on Monday because you will not find anything, you will need to make a list of appropriate places.

Time management

If you want to be successful you need to manage your time right. Most of the successful people manage their time right. 80% of results achieved are achieved by the top 20% of people, and that is because they manage their time right. Time management is the direction and control of the events in an effective and efficient way. Make a list of all the things you want to do and then prioritise.

> A must be done
> B should be done
> C could be done (not important)
> D delegate
> E eliminate

You will also need to focus on clear specific goals in order to achieve them.

Goal settings

There are thousands of books on goal settings and that is why I am not going to talk to you about goal achievement. Goals need to be your own, not some ones else. You cannot have some ones else goals that goal is for him/her. The goals need to be balanced, you cannot have goals which are about money only or personal development. Goals give you direction, a direction chosen by you. You will be a like a death fish in the water if you do not have goals. Why do you want the goal? This is more important than the goal. The goal can change the reason, stays the same. Make the written goals clear and specific e.g.: I increase my salary by 10 000 in the next month not I have more money. Only have 4 goals at the most. Everything more than that will send you in an anxiety attack. Not less than two goals the thinking will block the superconscious mind from getting through. Stay focused on the goal until you will achieve it. Be open minded. Ask, what if I do more of this? What if I do less of this? What if I do not do it at all? Use logic and analytical thinking to solve the problem, and if you cannot solve it, give it to the superconscious mind and get on with other problems. The above process is called acting intelligently which you can do even if you did not go to university. I urge to master it and use it all the time. The goal will meet you on your path to the goal. Also dwell on the goal and feel like you have it already. It will attract your goal faster. The goals need to match your values otherwise you will not feel satisfactions.

Human capacity to develop

Constructive attitudes when you take a constructive view and approach to life, to relationships, to work, to personal development etc. Most of the success is attitudinal from constructive attitudes. Self-concept is the bundle of beliefs, the master programme to your computer. Self-concept is made of self-esteem, self-ideal and self-image. Self-esteem is how you feel about yourself. To increase your self-esteem you say over and over 'I like myself more today than yesterday, and I like myself more tomorrow then today'. The self-esteem is measured by how much you love yourself how much you like yourself. Children come into this world with 'full potential'. They are spontaneous, are unafraid and uninhibited. When you achieve greatness you will be uninhibited and unafraid. To control their children parents use destructive criticism. Instead of controlling their children, constructive criticism develops two negative habits which create fear of failure and fear of rejection. Fear of failure leads to failure in life. Fear of rejection leads to conditional love. 'If you do not, you are going to get it', You are not loved until you do what we want you to do. Both these fears are destructive to life. Self-esteem is my favourite topic in personal development. And I think it will eventually be adopted by the whole world. Let's say in 100 years. Self-esteem is the core to your self-concept.

Catharsis and suppressed emotions

Catharsis is the re-experience of a traumatic event and expressing strong emotions associated with them. It is a safe expression of emotions. When I left the communist system for a capitalist one I had a traumatic experience. I used catharsis for this event and found a new way of thinking of the event and after the event. As you increase your self-esteem it will become easier and easier to get into event. The catharsis experiment will unblock your emotions and will allow new flow of energy. It will also allow you to look at the event with a different more healthy view. Expressing your emotions are a healthy way, but sometimes is not socially acceptable. You cannot get upset with your boss, you cannot get steam off at the soccer ground. To find a place to do it is very important. Women and men with unexpressed emotions are more vulnerable to depression and anxiety, during their life time. These people are also left with blockage of energy required for running their life. The key in dealing with repressed emotion is to accept them for what they are, emotions and energy. By accepting the feeling we feel at ease because there is no resistance. So, a much better way is too observe them rather than resist them. There is a limit of energy let out by emotions. Be calm and relaxed, eventually the pressure will run out and so do the repressed emotions. Another way in dealing with suppressed emotions is to express them in an accepting way. You can play an instrument which can be started at any age with one hour of play a day. I personally use the electric guitar I started playing at age of 19; too late to play in a band that was my belief. Anyway to have a successful band you require a lot of effort and energy. There are millions of guitars player in the world. Whenever I feel lonely or need to release some of the unexpressed emotions, I use the guitar. You can also paint if you like that, and it can be started at any age. You can go to the gym and do various sports if you are in a good shape. To express feelings of love you can always have a dog as a pet. Dogs are very good, but keep in mind they need attention and affection. You will get a lot of love in return. Personally, I prefer cats, because I do not have the time and energy and place to grow a dog.

Getting around the right people

It is not the people who help you but the right people you surround yourself with, that help you. Letting the right people on the bus is vital to your success. And this is regardless of where you are going. You will need to appreciate them and not be put off by the boredoms of the relationship. I had nice people, mirror people like me but never appreciated them and I lost them. Finding and keeping the right people is a vital step in your life. I hope you learn from me and do not repeat my mistakes. These right people will help you, protect from society which has a negative influence, like a wall of positive energy. It is very important to know that you are isolated by society's negative influences. By the power of suggestion you will get the colour of your environment. People who are positive, people who want to go somewhere, people who have goals and ideals like you. It is not going to be an easy task to find them, trust me I have been looking for a while. If you find him or her keep them, they are hard to find.

In your life there are 3 categories of people. People who are close to you and very influential. You spend a lot of time with them. People who you see once a week for a coffee with some level of influence. People who you meet once a month who do not influence you. People who you admire through magazines, brochures and publications, also have an influence on you, by the power of suggestion. Even if you only see them in the magazines.

Social Intelligence

I have covered so far relationships, intimate relationships and loving relationships. They are all part of the social intelligence package. Your ability to blend and get on with people. Social intelligence is the most important intelligence, since only by being with people you will achieve satisfactions and fulfilment in life. 85% of success is achieved with people. You will get kicked out of a few places and then you realize how good it is to get on well with others.

All my life I have had problems with people and is fair to say that only these days I get on well with people. My friendly nature has brought me to these days. Even if I feel good with people, the game of numbers is not for me. Since you I could not go further in life, I needed to learn the game of numbers. This game of numbers was probably developed thousands of years ago, I hate. Everybody sounds the same. Everybody has the same answers. Even the assertiveness of people is the same, or better said, there are only a finite number of models of assertiveness. With the word 'sorry' I always crack a joke so not to sound the same, regardless of people's age. Despite me not liking the game you will need to learn it, to know it well. It is very important in your ability to get on well with others. If you land in a group do not be the first or the last one, be in the middle that is the best policy and save you a lot of energy.

Also very important is to assert yours self, make sure you assert yourself, Also you may have a hard time doing it, but you need to do it. Until the age of 35 I did not do any assertiveness, I was living in my own world, withdrawn and shy. Make sure you know the people in the position of power, just to know how to deal with the situation. You also do not want to annoy them. The way on getting along with people is by the game of numbers. In a group of people, as soon as you meet them, stay back and let others do the talk. Until you find what they are really about and then integrate in the group. Be aware of people some are more external like Australians, some are more internal like me, and some are more balanced between external and internal. Your self-esteem will enhance your ability to get on well with others. (with self-esteem the less you fear anything). Enhancing someone else self-esteem will increase yours as well e.g.: 'you put so much effort into your job'. The compliment should be sincere and done immediately. If you are not sincere, people would pick up and that would not be a compliment. Practice some replies for yourself during the day. They will become very handy. Some people would practice in front of television. Be assertive and you get plenty of respect and they will let you stay there in their place. A nice and easy way of practising social skills is to have a group of people you meet every day of the week on different days. That will make you practice social skills. Also you should get a job in which you will get your social skills.

Something which I wanted to say is not to loose yourself in the game of numbers just because you practice it every day. After all it is only a game. And the more you accept it as a game, the better your life. Something you need to know is to hold your own, this is the ultimate goal in social intelligence.

Financial freedom and financial abundance

You need financial freedom so you do not get pushed around by the government and you have enough money to be free. You do not rely on the government money. I put this chapter at the end of the book because if you are not happy you will not enjoy the financial freedom. So, there is a requirement in the development stage. It is believed that more than a hundred thousand dollars will not make any difference on the happiness scale.

Some people are not interested in money, money does not make any difference to them. The truth is that money matters. You will need to buy food, health, books, trips and in general the good things in life. So, we perceive the financial freedom to be important. Another truth is that you see people with a lot of money not being happy or just happy a little bit. Or if they are running out of money they get back to being unhappy. And it is a good things because if you do not have money you can still be happy.

You will need to save money every week. Pay yourself in a savings account every time you get paid by the employer. Use an account without card so you cannot take out money every time you want. Only 5% of people save money, not to take into account the superannuation salary at 9.5% in Australia. Money that will not be enough for your retirement unless you start at an early age. Saving money is an achievement since only 5 % of people save money.

You need to know why you want financial freedom. You need to know what you need in order to have financial abundance. What contributions do you want to make in terms of finance. Personally financial freedom is not enough for me. It will not do it. I have high standards in terms of the house I want, the car I want, the holiday I want etc. Financial freedom will not do it. Earning 50 000$ a year will not do it. In the end I will probably rely on government money. To help people as well I need 100 million. 90 million for people who are entrepreneurs and need money to start new business. The money will be given as long as they have a good business proposition. For me there will be 10 million for the house and other expenses. This is what I want. Who knows? I might end up on the government pensions, but financial freedom will not do it. In Australia we save money 10% of the salary, compulsive in superannuation companies who invest the money. This money may be used at later stage in life in retirement to supplement the government pensions. In The Richest Man in Babylon by George Clayson, which I read years ago, they are talking about compounding where you put money into an account without you touching the money. He mentioned 10% to save and 10% to give away. In the beginning money grows slowly, but what happens when it gets a momentum? The money will increase exponentially. This is good for younger people but what happens when you are older.? You will need to become an investor or keep working until you die, 3 to 4 days a week. A good way to invest is in stock. In the stock market you do not lose money until you sell. People buy at low prices and sell at high prices. That is if the stock broker wants to buy the stock you recommend. The stock market is complicated especially in the area of puts, calls, options derivatives in general. Until they will make it simpler you will need qualifications in trading from the TAFE courses. Once you have this you will be able to trade every morning on computers without the need of a stock broker. You will learn mathematics and economics required to apply various financial systems. After 2 years of practice you will become an investor. This is one hour a day in the morning. I had the goal of trading a long time ago, but it never materialized. Maybe one day I will do it. I will do it because I have a good knowledge in mathematics. When you are young you can lose money and start over again. When you are older it is harder to start again money. What you will give away will come back, this is Karma. Be an investor but also give away money. One way to make money is to sell books, lots of them. A lot of people do that and become rich overnight. Although is a hard way to make money because there are millions of books being published. By the way, I do know where my money will come from.

And finally to have financial abundance you will need to spend less then you earn and invest the rest. You will need to:

> Define what you want in terms of money,
> Design an achievable plan to follow
> Be fully responsible, do not give away responsibility.

When it is tough keep going
Get a coach to help you

Relaxation

There are so many books on relaxation so I will not make a big deal about it. Current mindfulness is the meditation taken by a lot of people. It is a meditation in which you live for the moment. You will not have time for fear, because in the present there is no fear. I do it myself and is very good, that is the reason I added it to this book. Focus on the places of the body in the moment. E.g.my back lies on my bed, my head rests on the pillow. Also be aware of your environment the corner of the furniture is there, the bed seats on the floor etc. I hope you get the logic here. If you find yourself drifting, do not get upset, just go back to meditation and watch how you drifted. Another type of meditation I use is transcendental meditation. Align the body, mind and brain to work together. It is very good for relaxation. Focus on your breathing. Out or in or both kinds of breathing. The mind will wonder and you need to observe it and go back to meditation. Say' there is a thought' or 'there is an emotion.' With practice you will become good and you will be able to do short bursts meditation for 15 seconds. That is all it will take you to relax. Another type of meditation I use is tape affirmations with music. It relaxes the mind body and brain. So, the affirmations will be accepted very easily. With music in the background you can count from zero to twenty. Then you will get into a deep state of relaxation where you can listen to your affirmations. You can put anything on affirmations, gaining self-esteem would be a good one. Energy is another good one. There are more types of relaxation which you will find if you look for them.

The Process of Death

This subject can be easily placed after acquiring self-esteem, but I decided to put it last. Once you acquire self-esteem you will be able to go anywhere and cover various situations in your life. On the scale of development the process of death comes after the acquisition of self-esteem. Before you live, you need to die, before you die you need to live. So much truth in this statement taken from the bible. As is believed by many, the process of death is not about stopping to exist biologically. It is about living your life. What is that you want from life? If by any chance you live your life and get what you want from life you would not fear death. I lived my life, I have done the best I could with the knowledge at the time in my life. I have done what I was sent to do, now I can ascend to the next level. In general there would be something you did not achieve in this life. Again, how you deal with this is part of the process of death. A lot of people believe there is no life after death. That there is no higher level. If you think of the reason you were sent here you would realize there is another world. The soul never dies, the spirits exists, and the mind ascents and grows by acquiring total knowledge in this world. Plenty of reasons to believe there is another world. Another factor in the process of death is to believe that you have done your best with the knowledge at the time. It is easier to manage your life, when you think you have done your best. I was a good a father, I was a good worker, I was a good husband, I achieved my mission. Even if you have not achieved your mission, even the fact that you tried is something. The things which could not have been done, will be done in another world. You cannot stay in this world and do things over and over again, that is the comfort zone. There is also a natural emotion called boredom, so you will get bored after a while. To stay in the same relationship in this world would be unthinkable. What you will find in this world is moments and relationships which will not last. Another part of the process of death (or better said the process of life) is aging. Despite whatever opinion you have for yourself aging is a number. There is no difference between a healthy 20 year old and a 60 year individual. They can both do the same, provided they are healthy. The hair become silver in colour and the skin gets wrinkles. Do not equate wrinkles and silver hair with getting old it is not an appropriate definition. The eastern philosophy teachers equate aging with stopping to learn and grow. We are all here, in this world, for others with a mission. Until we change the world we are all here for others. It is a world of pain and that needs to be changed. Probably if you see animals put down at the abattoir so we can eat, you will probably not eat any meat. I know it takes a lot of energy and effort to be a vegetarian and even trees are probably hurting. Animals are not scared if you let them go by themselves to slaughter. It is when they are pushed to do things that makes them uncomfortable. Another reason you should not feel scared about dying is that it only takes place when you fulfil your mission. If you die without fulfilling your mission it is because you died living on the edge, driving formula 1 cars and going in a balloon around the world. In general people who die in the 80's or 90's are people who do not fulfil their mission and did not live on the edge. There can also be missions which take a long time to fulfil that is why people would live until late in their lives. You should also realize that dying biologically is part of living and it might happen. To recapitulate the process of death is the realisation that you did not live your life here (there is another world). It is easier to believe that there is another world, in order to deal with life. If you do not live on the edge, or you are not a free spirit (free spirit dies), you will die when you fulfil your mission. Accept yourself unconditionally, see yourself as a good father, as good worker etc. Do not believe in aging, it only happens when you stop learning.

3.0 Miscellaneous

Happiness

Is something that everybody wants no matter what stage of life they are at. The state of being happy is the ultimate goal of human beings and desired by everyone. One way to live your life is with so much joy, happiness and energy that you forget there is a past or a future. At most that is my desire. I might not be able to achieve that but I will pursue it no matter what happens. Happiness is a daily state of your system. It is the feeling of being happy.

Music therapy

We mentioned in the book that you do affirmations with music. That would balance the brain, the left side with the right side, you will feel calm and tranquil. One way to be calm is through music. If you read a book with music in the background, you will do a lot of reading into a calm state. Relaxation music is part of music therapy. There is also music uplifting and energy for the soul. The music should be without words. Expressing your feelings through an instrument is again music therapy. Music helps you to stay on positive not on negative emotions. The right music can give you rhythm and then you can do a lot of things. There is a lot of material if you want to continue with music therapy.

Social anxiety

Social anxiety is a fear that you are criticised, evaluated or judged by others. It can become more serious and you will develop social phobia. Shyness can become a social anxiety if it is not unbearable. In shyness we will have a feeling of self-consciousness, what would people think about me? Typical trigger thoughts in social anxiety are: 'Hi, he is looking at me', 'He or she thinks I am not worthy', 'Hi, what am I going to do'? (I am getting evaluated). No matter what others may say social anxiety is a form of performance anxiety, where you do not know how to handle the situation, when you do not know what to say, and how to behave. In order to deal with social anxiety you will need to start with one person, practicing your social skills. With a bit of anti-anxiety medication such as Paroxetine known as SSRI anti- depressants (paroxetine is good because it does not mask the cognitive thinking, it takes the edge off fear) you will be able to handle social situations. The cognitive thoughts associated with social phobias need to be replaced by more helpful ones. If you handle the situation with one person you should be able to handle the situations with many people. We live in a society where performance is seen every day. A society of 'stars' made by people, 'stars' which perform. If you have been suffering from social anxiety in isolation it will take a while to be sociable with everybody. I do not have to talk let the others start and do the talking. Talking is learned. Once I encounter the situation I will be better at it. The main point is to assert yourself.

Unfinished business

Unfinished business is relationships which are finished but you still hang on to them. Relationships with your ex-boss, with the member of the opposite sex or even the same sex. You still feel about that person and you are angry and hurt by him/her. You are entitled to anger and hurt by holding on to it. For long times it is not healthy for everybody. You can write a letter and burn it, so you will let go of hurt and anger.

It is selfish and appropriate to write a letter. If burning once the letter does not help, try burning it more times. It takes a while getting it out of the system.

Dear X,

I hate you because you hurt me. You hurt me by leaving me out (or any reasons the person did it to you). You hurt me by not talking to me. Despite all these I forgive you and let you go. I forgive you because you are stupid and do not understand that I am a worthy and valuable human being. I am worthy because God says so. In the face of God we are all worthy and valuable human beings. I forgive you and let you go. You are free and I am free. Now burn the letter and the anger and hurt should be diminished.

Some people say you should write the letter and mail the letter. But you do not want the other person to be involved. Other things that might help is to look at the other person's negative points, this makes it easier to forget.

Free Spirit

Would you like to be a free spirit? Maybe you do, so enjoy going from one person to others on any social strata. From prostitutes to CEO of companies. You will enjoy their company and also learning from them. Free spirit. The only problem with free spirit is that you will not be able to stay alive. The sooner you get away from the free spirit the better.

Habits

We are creatures of habit and what we do over and over again becomes a habit. Good healthy habits versus the negative habits which do not help us. Always develop a habit of being positive. Always look for the good in everything. This is good for your mental health. Habits of saving and investing money are good for your financial situation. The habit of getting up in the morning doing your affirmations and review your goals. Develop as many good habits as you can.

Fights

Is it fair and healthy to say that we fight amongst ourselves? In a world where life is short is fighting appropriate? Unfortunately even if you stop fighting the fact that the world is fighting, we cannot get away from it. It is advisable that you learn how to fight and pick the fights you want or think are appropriate. Do not fight with everybody like some people do. Picking your own fights is the right attitude. There are people who, if they stop fighting do not know what else they can do in their life. Similarly for people who get you, once they have got you and you accept them and they look for a different challenge, in other people. People do not know how to live. This is the ego talking.

Main stream versus supportive stream

There are two streams in this world. The supportive people who support the main stream and the supported stream the main stream of people. Without the supportive stream the main stream would not exist. The supportive stream builds institutions, organisations, companies, etc. everything which is required for human existence. In Australia 70% of people are the supported, and 30% are the supportive, this is because there are migrants involved in the building of the country. In the world in general the ratio is 35% to 65%. The main stream of people make a living are pumping up their ego and scared about loosing their lives. Some of the people in the stream are mixing with each other. You need to know how to deal with each stream. Of particular interest are the one-dimensionals, people who will only have one dimension and do things because they have to. Some of them are simpleton, they see things simple even if they are not. They will enter the supportive stream to get dimensions from those.

Dwell on what you want

If you dwell on what you want you will not have time for fear. And by attractions you will achieve your goal. One emotion will dominate the other emotions so keep to the positive ones.

Take your opportunities

If you are a great man, a lot of life time opportunities will be facing you. Picking ones which are right for you and letting go off others is the challenge for you. The ones right for you means those which match your passion and what you could become the best in the world and your economic denominator if you have one. The more dimension you have the more opportunities you will get. If you are not a great man lifetime opportunities and opportunities in general should be taken. It will make life easier and give you new directions. If you have more dimensions you will work better with the superconscious mind. Acquisition of dimension will be the business of life if marriages are not for you. It means you are on a path of completeness.

Visualization

Despite what many people would say, visualization is not good for your life, particularly if you are prone to anxiety. The brain will give you unhappy pictures and you will need to shake your head to get rid of them. They will also block your superconscious solutions. Instead of visualization, imagining the feeling will have a better effect.

Attitude

85% of success is attitudinal. As I mentioned before Constructive attitude is a way of looking at the situation constructively. There are attitudes which are constructive versus the ones which are destructive. Constructive attitudes towards your work, relationships, personal development, mission, people, life etc. are the key to a positive mental health. Today in society a lot of people are destructive and they look to put not much in the system but to get a lot which of course does not work.

Good leaders

I brought up this chapter about enduring great leaders because they are not many. However the more they are the bigger the contribution to changing the world and the better for the human race. I have to admit that great leaders are probably born that way. I am not an expert in leadership, I want to make a point about great leaders. Some of the qualities of good leaders are: commitment and passion, good communication, decision making capabilities, creativity and innovativeness, accountability, delegation and empowerment, confidence, honesty and integrity. He or she needs to inspire others and need to have empathy. According to Jim Collins in his book 'From good to great', he or she will need to be also an effective leader, a competent manager, a contributing team member and a highly capable individual. Not in this order but all the qualities need to be explored. He needs to be humble and fearless/ modest and wilful.

Seriousness

Do not take your life too seriously, loosen up. We mentioned in the book that you change embarrass to amuse, and it is so true. The only thing serious is 'control' and life. Life is not a rehearsal, this is it. But taking things too seriously, being hard on yourself is not the way to go. You are more successful if you see the fun out of the situation. Also amuse yourself. What is better to amuse yourself than human stupidity. Human stupidity was put into this world at birth. So, this is how you were meant to be. Amusing yourself every day. Einstein once said: 'Human stupidity and space are infinite but I do not know about space'. It is so true. But as I said it is an instrument with which you have fun every day. Until we learned we are all stupid. So, you also need to face your stupidity and at the same time learn. If by any chance you are suffering of CFS 'standard' you can use the affirmations given to you in the book and be happy. At least for a couple of hours, after you wake up. Affirmations said before you go to bed, are then picked up by the hypnopompic state. You have enough information to be happy for some time. Some people would say, go to the supermarket and slap somebody on the bottom. This is to take you out of the comfort zone so, you get a bit of fear. Do not fear anything because the people are not going to do anything to you. What I also recommend, and you will be able to do it, when you go home and are by yourself rehearse your good time moments so this will double your moments in the day. In this way you are multiplying your good moments. Usually people rehearse the bad times so fear is taking time. We change this to the positive experiences. I used this technique myself for a long time, and for some reasons dropped it. It is no longer in my repertoire. So, I consider this as a fact of life. Since the supreme goal of human beings is to be happy, I hope you will apply it to you. There are people who say you cannot be happy until you get rid of ignorance. It is not true, you can be happy and ignorant, you are on your way to lose your ignorance.

Falling asleep

We assume that you do not have any problems with your sleep despite the fact that 50% of the population has a sleeping problem. If you cannot fall asleep you can read a book. In many cases it helps. But if you say to yourself allowed "I lay down in bed and fall sleep' just as you are in bed and try to get to sleep you will fall asleep. I have done this for years and this has worked with no problems.

Support Group

If you do everything and you are comfortable with the level of development you achieved, but things do not go well, you will probably need support. Support groups for which these books are good, will help you a lot. You are on your road to full potential with lots of dimensions. The more dimensions you have the more likely you are to work with the superconscious mind and God. Working with the superconscious mind and God will be easily done because you are complete. At the support group you will need to find the person with which you connect. The person who will be there for you and the person who will be there for themselves. If by any chance you do not find him/her keep trying. Do the shopping until you find the right merchandise, until you find the right person.

I tried to write this book as a stepping stone to personal development. Initially I tried to make it complete manual but this was not possible. I tried to write this book so people suffering of Chronic Fatigue Syndrome can cure themselves. I am more concerned about the extreme cases because this is where people are taking their lives. Also doctors who do not know and are convinced that CFS does not exists will be convinced following reading of the book of the destructiveness of the condition. It is a condition where the mind plays a significant role, be in the shutting down of the system or the anxiety layers attach to it. No matter how hard the condition is, it is curable around a life style of savings energies. And savings lives is a good business of life.